TO

FROM

DATE

MY FIRST GRATITUDE JOURNAL

Rejoice always. I Thess. 5:16

DaySpring

LIVE YOUR FAITH

DATE:

Today I'm grateful for...

I'm grateful because...

Thank you, God, for...

Stare at the shapes, then turn them into things that God made. When you're done, circle the creation you're the most grateful for.

DATE:

Today I'm grateful for...

I'm grateful because...

Thank you, God, for...

How grateful do you usually feel throughout your day? Fill in this pie chart to see a visual of how *grateful*, *ungrateful*, or *neutral* you feel.

Here's an example →

○ Grateful ○ ungrateful ○ Neutral

BONUS Ask a trusted friend or family member if they agree with the way you filled out your chart.

DATE:

Today I'm grateful for...

I'm grateful because...

Thank you, God, for...

Circle the season it is right now:

WINTER SPRING SUMMER FALL

Now fill in the blanks below
to write about the season you're in!

I'm grateful for all the seasons God gives us, and now it's ____________. During this season, the weather where I live in ____________ is ____________.

I enjoy going outside to ____________.

My favorite things about this season are ____________ and ____________.

I can show ____________ to others this season by ____________. I'm extra grateful for ____________ during this time of the year.

DATE:

Today I'm grateful for...

I'm grateful because...

Thank you, God, for...

Print/write/color the word "Thanks" in as many ways as you can imagine.

THANKS

Enter His gates with thanksgiving;
go into His courts with praise.
Give thanks to Him and praise His name.

PSALM 100:4 NLT

DATE:

Today I'm grateful for...

I'm grateful because...

Thank you, God, for...

We have five senses, and smell is the one that's said to be most strongly connected to our memories. Maybe you love the smell of warm cookies, freshly cut grass, your grandma's perfume, or your favorite flower.

What are 3–4 different scents you are grateful for? Write them out here and think about any memories you have with those smells.

DATE:

Today I'm grateful for...

I'm grateful because...

Thank you, God, for...

Add details to the city scene below. We already started a few.
Think windows, leaves, awnings, birds in the sky, people, etc.

DATE:

Today I'm grateful for...

I'm grateful because...

Thank you, God, for...

Lots of things can get in the way of practicing gratitude.

What keeps you from feeling grateful?

Circle as many things in the list as you want.

1. Being jealous of others
2. Feeling worried or anxious
3. Thinking about what you don't have
4. Being too busy
5. Other people with ungrateful attitudes
6. Focusing on negative things
7. Other ______________________

The next time you're feeling ungrateful because of any of the reasons above, what could you do to choose gratitude instead?

Write out one or two ideas.

DATE:

Today I'm grateful for...

I'm grateful because...

Thank you, God, for...

Which sea creature are you the most grateful for?

STARFISH SHARK BLOWFISH DOLPHIN SEA HORSE

STINGRAY CRAB LOBSTER WHALE TORTOISE

Draw and color a doodle of whichever creature you chose!

DATE:

Today I'm grateful for...

I'm grateful because...

Thank you, God, for...

Finish adding the details to these houses.
Think windows, siding, bricks, chimneys, solar panels,
rock, shutters, shingles, shrubs, etc.

There are many rooms in My Father's house;
I would not tell you this if it were not true. I am going there
to prepare a place for you, I will come back and take you
to be with Me so that you may be where I am.

JOHN 14:2-3 NCV

DATE:

Today I'm grateful for...

I'm grateful because...

Thank you, God, for...

Write out a prayer thanking God for whatever you wrote in your journaling section today. Add some color and doodles around the words you write.

DATE:

Today I'm grateful for...

I'm grateful because...

Thank you, God, for...

How many words can you make from this phrase?

I CAN BE GRATEFUL.

DATE:

Today I'm grateful for...

I'm grateful because...

Thank you, God, for...

Doodle some plants and trees that haven't been discovered yet. Add some fruits and name them.

Then God said, "Let the land sprout with vegetation—every sort of seed-bearing plant, and trees that grow seed-bearing fruit. These seeds will then produce the kinds of plants and trees from which they came." And that is what happened.

GENESIS 1:11 NLT

DATE:

Today I'm grateful for...

I'm grateful because...

Thank you, God, for...

Read this Psalm of Thanksgiving.
Underline any words or phrases that stand out to you.

Shout with joy to the LORD, all the earth!
Worship the LORD with gladness.
Come before Him, singing with joy.
Acknowledge that the LORD is God!
He made us, and we are His.
We are His people, the sheep of His pasture.
Enter His gates with thanksgiving;
go into His courts with praise.
Give thanks to Him and praise His name.
For the LORD is good.
His unfailing love continues forever,
and His faithfulness continues to each generation.

Psalm 100 NLT

DATE:

Today I'm grateful for...

I'm grateful because...

Thank you, God, for...

Color, draw, or doodle in the details to the planets.

I praise You because You made me
in an amazing and wonderful way.
What You have done is wonderful.
I know this very well.

PSALM 139:14 ICB

DATE:

Today I'm grateful for...

I'm grateful because...

Thank you, God, for...

Add more birds singing in the rain.

Then God said,
". . . Let the skies be filled with birds of every kind."
GENESIS 1:20 NLT

DATE:

Today I'm grateful for...

I'm grateful because...

Thank you, God, for...

Look at the colors below. Write one thing that you are grateful for to go with each color. Example: red = apples.

DATE:

Today I'm grateful for...

I'm grateful because...

Thank you, God, for...

Circle the things in this list that you feel especially grateful for today. Then pray and thank God for whatever you circled.

FRIENDS

FAMILY

SCHOOL

PETS

FOOD

WATER

GAMES

MUSIC

YOUR HOME

THE WEATHER

DATE:

Today I'm grateful for...

I'm grateful because...

Thank you, God, for...

Draw in the faces, shapes, and patterns on the emojis.

I will forget my complaint, change my expression, and smile.

JOB 9:27 CSB

DATE:

Today I'm grateful for...

I'm grateful because...

Thank you, God, for...

What are you grateful for when you think about your past?
In the space below, write 3–4 sentences about
one of your favorite memories from the last few years.
You can include details like your age,
where the memory took place, and the emotions you felt.

DATE:

Today I'm grateful for...

I'm grateful because...

Thank you, God, for...

Finish drawing a few of the cats and draw more too. You can also color them. Orange cats, white cats, black cats, striped cats, etc.

DATE:

Today I'm grateful for...

I'm grateful because...

Thank you, God, for...

Unscramble the underlined words in this Bible verse. Write the correct words in the blanks to complete the verse.

HTSI IS THE AYD
THE DLOD HAS MDEA.
WE WILL ICORJEE
AND BE LDAG IN IT.
ALPSM 118:24 NLT

____ IS THE ___
THE ____ HAS ____.
WE WILL _______
AND BE ____ IN IT.
_____ 118:24 NLT

DATE:

Today I'm grateful for...

I'm grateful because...

Thank you, God, for...

Look around you. List four people, places, or things you can see right now that you are grateful for. Draw simple sketches of everything on your list.

DATE:

Today I'm grateful for...

I'm grateful because...

Thank you, God, for...

Draw what you see in the shape of these clouds.

Then everyone will see the Son of Man
coming on a cloud with power and great glory.

LUKE 21:27 NLT

DATE:

Today I'm grateful for...

I'm grateful because...

Thank you, God, for...

What characteristics of God are you especially thankful for?

Circle the ones in this list that stand out.

Then pray and thank God for who He is!

POWERFUL	FAITHFUL
KIND	WISE
LOVING	JUST
GOOD	HOLY
ALL-KNOWING	MERCIFUL
FORGIVING	GRACE-GIVING

DATE:

Today I'm grateful for...

I'm grateful because...

Thank you, God, for...

Write a few sentences about a place you are grateful for below. Maybe it's a certain city, someone's home, or any other place you love to visit.

DATE:

Today I'm grateful for...

I'm grateful because...

Thank you, God, for...

Fill this page with crosses. Big, little, smooth, rugged, colored, etc. As you do, think about Jesus and all He's done for you!

Never boast about anything except
the cross of our Lord Jesus Christ.

GALATIANS 6:14 NLT

DATE:

Today I'm grateful for...

I'm grateful because...

Thank you, God, for...

Write things you are thankful for today inside the leaves on this tree.

DATE:

Today I'm grateful for...

I'm grateful because...

Thank you, God, for...

Write what you're thankful for on the sidewalk.

(you can even decorate with sidewalk chalk.)

DATE:

Today I'm grateful for...

I'm grateful because...

Thank you, God, for...

What article of clothing are you the most thankful for?

Draw a simple doodle of you wearing whatever it is below.

DATE:

Today I'm grateful for...

I'm grateful because...

Thank you, God, for...

Write a list of people you are grateful for in the first column. In the second column, circle the face emoji that best represents how well you show them your gratitude.

NAME

DATE:

Today I'm grateful for...

I'm grateful because...

Thank you, God, for...

Take the list of the people you're thankful for from the previous day and write their names in the first column. In the next column, write why you are thankful for them. In the third column write an idea about how you could show gratitude toward them.

Name	Why I am Thankful for them	How I will Show gratitude

DATE:

Today I'm grateful for...

I'm grateful because...

Thank you, God, for...

Draw faces of people who make your life brighter and happier. It could be family, friends, teachers, or anyone special to you. Write something you're thankful for next to each face.

For we are God's masterpiece.

EPHESIANS 2:10 NLT

DATE:

Today I'm grateful for...

I'm grateful because...

Thank you, God, for...

Brain dump! Set a timer for three minutes and write as many things as you can think of that you are grateful for today on this page.

DATE:

Today I'm grateful for...

I'm grateful because...

Thank you, God, for...

Draw musical instruments, create your own instruments, and add anything musical such as boombox, earbuds, etc. You may even want to try writing a song or melody.

Sing and make music from your heart to the Lord, always giving thanks to God the Father for everything, in the name of our Lord Jesus Christ.

EPHESIANS 5:19–20 NIV

DATE:

Today I'm grateful for...

I'm grateful because...

Thank you, God, for...

Write a thankfulness prayer to God by filling in the blanks.

DEAR GOD,

THANK YOU FOR ____________________ ME. YOU HAVE GIVEN US LOTS OF THINGS TO BE GRATEFUL FOR. THANK YOU FOR GIVING ME ____________________ BECAUSE ____________________. I'M GLAD YOU MADE ____________________ SO THAT I ____________________.

I'M THANKFUL THAT I CAN TALK TO YOU ABOUT ____________________. PLEASE HELP ME SHOW MY GRATITUDE TO OTHERS THIS WEEK BY ____________________.

AMEN.

DATE:

Today I'm grateful for...

I'm grateful because...

Thank you, God, for...

Draw a picture of a friend you're feeling extra grateful for today.

As iron sharpens iron, so a friend sharpens a friend.

PROVERBS 27:17 NLT

DATE:

Today I'm grateful for...

I'm grateful because...

Thank you, God, for...

Take this journal outside with you
(or find a window if you can't go outside)
and write down all the things you see that you're grateful for.

DATE:

Today I'm grateful for...

I'm grateful because...

Thank you, God, for...

Fill the insides of these clocks with things the Lord has been right on time with in your life.

Let's not get tired of doing what is good.
At just the right time we will reap a harvest of blessing
if we don't give up.

GALATIANS 6:9 NLT

DATE:

Today I'm grateful for...

I'm grateful because...

Thank you, God, for...

Rewrite this song of praise from the book of Psalms:

Come, let us sing to the Lord!
Let us shout joyfully to the Rock of our salvation.
Let us come to Him with thanksgiving.
Let us sing psalms of praise to Him.
For the Lord is a great God,
a great King above all gods.

PSALM 95:1–3 NLT

DATE:

Today I'm grateful for...

I'm grateful because...

Thank you, God, for...

Draw happy faces on the kids on the school bus along with your favorite school supplies and everything that makes your school days special. Draw each item with gratitude, thinking about how they help you learn and have fun.

In all the work you are doing, work the best you can.
Work as if you were working for the Lord, not for men.

COLOSSIANS 3:23 ICB

DATE:

Today I'm grateful for...

I'm grateful because...

Thank you, God, for...

Draw a doodle of your favorite meal.

Did someone make this meal for you?

If so, tell them "Thank you" the next time you see them.

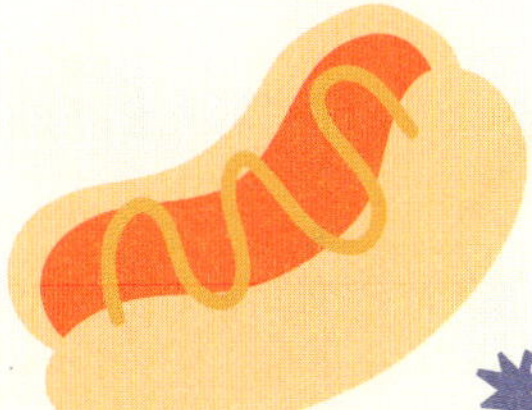

DATE:

Today I'm grateful for...

I'm grateful because...

Thank you, God, for...

Ask friends and family members
to tell you what they're grateful for.

Name: Grateful for:

DATE:

Today I'm grateful for...

I'm grateful because...

Thank you, God, for...

Embark on a gratitude adventure maze! Imagine you're a kind hiker who got lost in the maze of thoughts. Each twist and turn represents something you're thankful for. Draw a path through the maze, connecting the hiker to the things you appreciate. Maybe it's family, friends, pets, or special moments. Write or draw a symbol in each section to represent your gratitude. Guide the hiker through the maze of thankfulness, helping them find their way back home to a heart full of gratitude.

DATE:

Today I'm grateful for...

I'm grateful because...

Thank you, God, for...

What are some of your favorite sounds? Maybe it's a song you love, a special person's laugh, or the crackling of crunchy fall leaves. Write a few sentences about one or two of your favorite sounds and why you are grateful for them.

DATE:

Today I'm grateful for...

I'm grateful because...

Thank you, God, for...

Fill up this gratitude jar image with words or doodles of things you're grateful for.

BONUS

Create a real-life gratitude jar!

Put slips of paper inside a jar and write down the things from this list on the paper. The next time you're feeling down, take out your jar and look through all the things you're grateful for—and maybe even add some more.

DATE:

Today I'm grateful for...

I'm grateful because...

Thank you, God, for...

Draw or write a memory of some of your favorite photos.

I thank God every time I remember you.

PHILIPPIANS 1:3 ICB

DATE:

Today I'm grateful for...

I'm grateful because...

Thank you, God, for...

Read the story of creation in Genesis 1–2.
Write down some of the things God created.
Draw a doodle of the thing you're feeling
the most grateful for in God's creation today.

DATE:

Today I'm grateful for...

I'm grateful because...

Thank you, God, for...

Go on a walk, even if it's just around your home. Keep track of things you see that you're grateful for and write down the top three.

1.

2.

3.

DATE:

Today I'm grateful for...

I'm grateful because...

Thank you, God, for...

Try drawing the dinosaurs shown.
Color them in or create patterns on them.

Everything God created is good.

I TIMOTHY 4:4 THE MESSAGE

DATE:

Today I'm grateful for...

I'm grateful because...

Thank you, God, for...

God gives us the gift of sleep! Maybe you haven't thought about sleep as a gift, but it's something we can thank God for. Read this verse and write down something you're grateful for when it comes to sleep.

In peace I will lie down and sleep,
for You alone, O Lord, will keep me safe.

PSALM 4:8 NLT

DATE:

Today I'm grateful for...

I'm grateful because...

Thank you, God, for...

Fill in the rest of these faces and draw in the hairstyles.

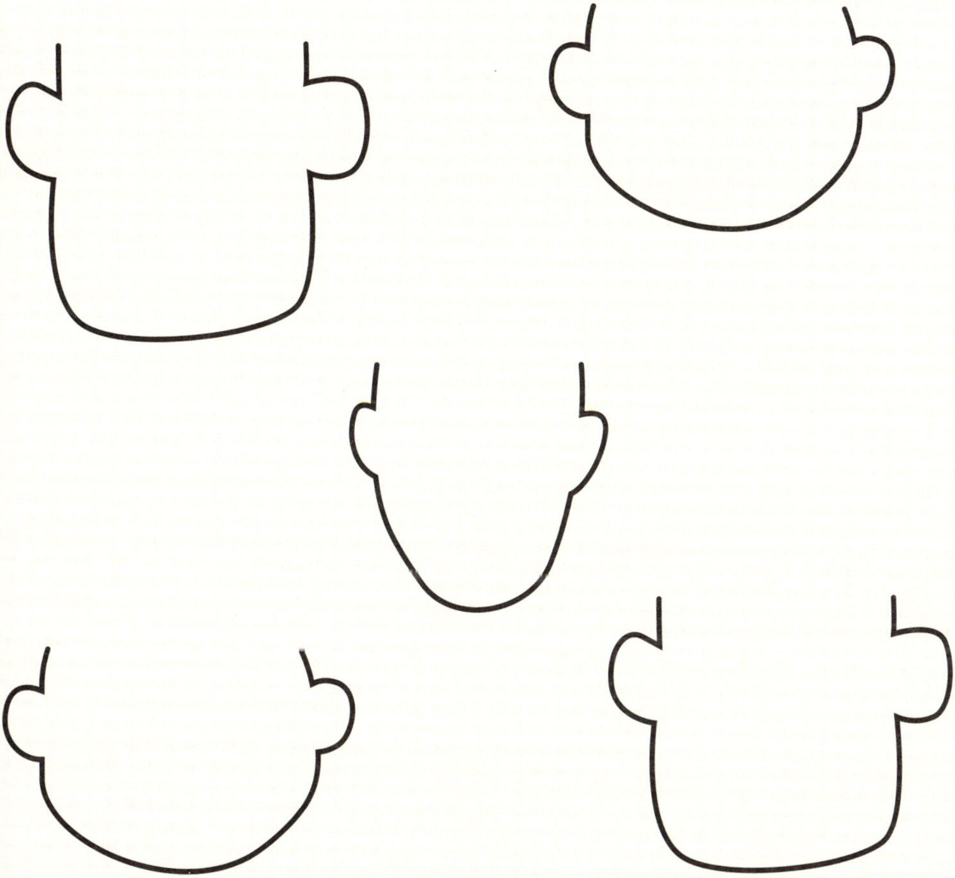

[God] pays . . . attention to you, down to the last detail—even numbering the hairs on your head!

MATTHEW 10:29 THE MESSAGE

DATE:

Today I'm grateful for...

I'm grateful because...

Thank you, God, for...

Color this goose riding a bike as you think about something silly that you're grateful for.

P.S. Does this picture look familiar? :)

DATE:

Today I'm grateful for...

I'm grateful because...

Thank you, God, for...

Whether you love school or not, you probably have at least one school subject or activity you're grateful for. Write down what you're the most grateful for about school.

BONUS

Say "thank you" to your teacher(s) and tell them what you wrote here!

DATE:

Today I'm grateful for...

I'm grateful because...

Thank you, God, for...

Picture a world where friendly monsters and delicious cookies come together in the spirit of gratitude. Draw lovable monsters and scrumptious cookies below, each representing something you are thankful for.

DATE:

Today I'm grateful for...

I'm grateful because...

Thank you, God, for...

Circle which forest animal you are the most thankful for.

BUNNY BEAR HEDGEHOG SQUIRREL RACCOON

FOX CHIPMUNK BIRD MOOSE WOLF

Next, draw and color a picture of that animal in its natural habitat.

DATE:

Today I'm grateful for...

I'm grateful because...

Thank you, God, for...

Turn these blobs into birds.

Look at the birds. They don't plant or harvest or store food in barns, for your heavenly Father feeds them. And aren't you far more valuable to Him than they are?

MATTHEW 6:26 NLT

DATE:

Today I'm grateful for...

I'm grateful because...

Thank you, God, for...

What are two items that you can touch right now? Write down how they feel. Are you thankful for these items? Why or why not?

DATE:

Today I'm grateful for...

I'm grateful because...

Thank you, God, for...

Play Gratitude Tic-Tac-Toe! Find someone to play with you. Before you write your X or your O, you need to say something you're grateful for about the other person.

DATE:

Today I'm grateful for...

I'm grateful because...

Thank you, God, for...

As you color the robot below and fill the page with more robots, consider the ways technology makes your life better—whether it's helping with school, connecting with friends and family, or providing exciting entertainment.

DATE:

Today I'm grateful for...

I'm grateful because...

Thank you, God, for...

Gratitude check! How thankful are you feeling today? Circle the face emoji that best represents your level of gratitude. Write down a few sentences about why you think you're feeling this way.

DATE:

Today I'm grateful for...

I'm grateful because...

Thank you, God, for...

How many words can you make from this phrase?

I AM THANKFUL TODAY

DATE:

Today I'm grateful for...

I'm grateful because...

Thank you, God, for...

Imagine a vibrant swimming pool scene! Draw and color the pool, the sparkling water, colorful floaties, lounge chairs, umbrellas, and maybe even a snack bar. Add labels or small notes expressing your gratitude for each element.

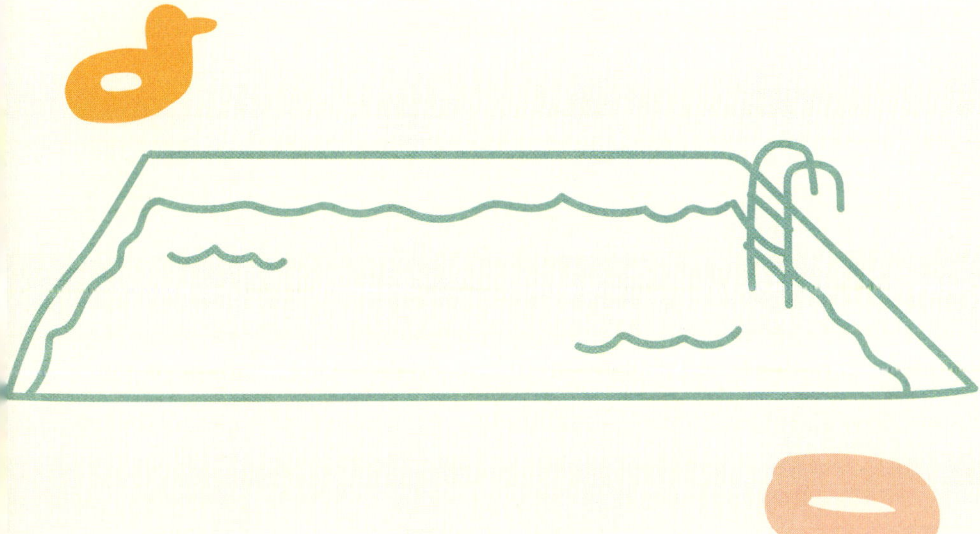

DATE:

Today I'm grateful for...

I'm grateful because...

Thank you, God, for...

Write a note of gratitude to a leader in your life like a teacher, pastor, or coach. Use the space on this page as your rough draft, and then write it out again on a notecard or sheet of paper so you can give it to that person. It could make their day!

DATE:

Today I'm grateful for...

I'm grateful because...

Thank you, God, for...

Trace your hand below. Even if it's nowhere near Thanksgiving, turn your hand tracing into a cute turkey!

DATE:

Today I'm grateful for...

I'm grateful because...

Thank you, God, for...

Draw and color different kinds of trees and plants.
Feel free to make them up.

The person who trusts in the LORD will be blessed. . . . He will be strong, like a tree planted near water. That tree has large roots that find the water. It is not afraid when the days are hot. Its leaves are always green. It does not worry in a year when no rain comes. That tree always produces fruit.

JEREMIAH 17:7–8 ICB

DATE:

Today I'm grateful for...

I'm grateful because...

Thank you, God, for...

Choose a person in your life you see often.
Write down five reasons why you are grateful for this person.
Then go show them this list!

Name:

1.

2.

3.

4.

5.

DATE:

Today I'm grateful for...

I'm grateful because...

Thank you, God, for...

you can be grateful from A–Z! Write down something you are grateful for that starts with each letter of the alphabet. We'll just go through the letter M today.

A ______________________________

B ______________________________

C ______________________________

D ______________________________

E ______________________________

F ______________________________

G ______________________________

H ______________________________

I ______________________________

J ______________________________

K ______________________________

L ______________________________

M ______________________________

DATE:

Today I'm grateful for...

I'm grateful because...

Thank you, God, for...

We're continuing the A–Z gratitude list from yesterday. Write down something you are grateful for that starts with the letter N all the way to Z!

N ______________________________

O ______________________________

P ______________________________

Q ______________________________

R ______________________________

S ______________________________

T ______________________________

U ______________________________

V ______________________________

W ______________________________

X ______________________________

Y ______________________________

Z ______________________________

DATE:

Today I'm grateful for...

I'm grateful because...

Thank you, God, for...

Doodle impossible things. Dream up new creatures, enchanted lands, original superheroes, and fun gadgets and inventions. And as you do, celebrate the joy of creativity and the incredible power of your imagination.

I am the LORD, the God of every person on the earth. Nothing is impossible for Me.

JEREMIAH 32:27 NCV

DATE:

Today I'm grateful for...

I'm grateful because...

Thank you, God, for...

Read this story about the time when Jesus healed ten men with leprosy.

As Jesus continued on toward Jerusalem, He reached the border between Galilee and Samaria. As He entered a village there, ten men with leprosy stood at a distance, crying out, "Jesus, Master, have mercy on us!" He looked at them and said, "Go show yourselves to the priests." And as they went, they were cleansed of their leprosy. One of them, when he saw that he was healed, came back to Jesus, shouting, "Praise God!" He fell to the ground at Jesus' feet, thanking Him for what he had done. This man was a Samaritan. Jesus asked, "Didn't I heal ten men? Where are the other nine? Has no one returned to give glory to God except this foreigner?" And Jesus said to the man, "Stand up and go. Your faith has healed you."

LUKE 17:11-19 NLT

Do you think you are more like the one man who thanked Jesus or the other nine? What could you thank Jesus for right now?

DATE:

Today I'm grateful for...

I'm grateful because...

Thank you, God, for...

How many times has a dog brought joy to your life? Whether it be a pet who sleeps in the bed with you every night, or a dog who lives in your neighborhood, or a puppy you got to pet last week at the park—dogs can always find a way to lift your spirits! Finish out the details in the doggies and while you do, think through all the ways dogs have brought happiness and laughter to your life.

DATE:

Today I'm grateful for...

I'm grateful because...

Thank you, God, for...

What's your favorite season? Draw and color doodles of some things you're especially thankful for when this season comes around!

DATE:

Today I'm grateful for...

I'm grateful because...

Thank you, God, for...

Read this verse from the book of John out loud.

For God so loved the world that He gave
His one and only Son, that whoever believes in Him
shall not perish but have eternal life.

JOHN 3:16 NIV

God sent Jesus because He loves you! Isn't that amazing?
Write out a prayer to God thanking Him for sending Jesus for us.

DATE:

Today I'm grateful for...

I'm grateful because...

Thank you, God, for...

Create a garden of gratitude! Decorate each flowerpot to represent one good thing God has given you. Good things could include your family, friends, nature, favorite foods, your home, sunshine, and so much more! Don't forget to add flowers!

Yes, there will be an abundance of flowers and singing and joy! . . . There the Lord will display His glory, the splendor of our God.

ISAIAH 35:2 NLT

DATE:

Today I'm grateful for...

I'm grateful because...

Thank you, God, for...

Circle the safari animal you're the most grateful for.

GIRAFFE LION TIGER FLAMINGO

ELEPHANT WARTHOG CHEETAH MONKEY

HIPPOPOTAMUS OSTRICH

Then write a few sentences about what you'd think it would be like to have this animal as a pet!

DATE:

Today I'm grateful for...

I'm grateful because...

Thank you, God, for...

Find your way to the treasure chest.

List 5 treasures in your life.

1.________________ 2.________________

3.________________ 4.________________

5.________________

Store up for yourselves treasures in heaven. . . .
For where your treasure is, there your heart will be.

MATTHEW 6:20–21 CSB

DATE:

Today I'm grateful for...

I'm grateful because...

Thank you, God, for...

Unscramble the underlined words in this Bible verse.
Write the correct words in the blanks to complete the verse.

GIVE NSHTKA
TO THE ORDL,
FOR HE IS OODG!
HIS HFUFTLIA VELO
ENDURES ROFERVE.
PSALM 107:1 NLT

GIVE ______
TO THE ____
FOR HE IS ____!
HIS _________ ____
ENDURES _______.
PSALM 107:1 NLT

DATE:

Today I'm grateful for...

I'm grateful because...

Thank you, God, for...

It's fun to create pretend kingdoms and to dream of being kings, queens, princes, and princesses. Was there ever a time in your life when you felt special? Maybe it was your birthday or a holiday or the awards assembly at school? As you draw crowns, tiaras, and jewels below, think about how this special event made you feel, and how much you are truly valued by God and so many others! Don't forget to add the palace!

Jesus said, "Let the little children come to Me.
Don't stop them, because the kingdom of heaven belongs
to people who are like these children."

MATTHEW 19:14 ICB

DATE:

Today I'm grateful for...

I'm grateful because...

Thank you, God, for...

Fill in the blanks to write a note about a family member you're grateful for.

I am grateful for ____________________ because ____________________. I love when ____________ and I ____________________ together. My favorite qualities about ____________ are ____________________ and ____________________. I'd like to show ____________________ that I am thankful for him/her by ____.

DATE:

Today I'm grateful for...

I'm grateful because...

Thank you, God, for...

Fill in your family tree, and as you do, thank God for each family member you list, and pray for them.

Generation after generation stands in awe of your work;
each one tells stories of your mighty acts.

PSALM 145:4 THE MESSAGE

DATE:

Today I'm grateful for...

I'm grateful because...

Thank you, God, for...

Doodle a picture of yourself doing an activity you're grateful for. Maybe it's your favorite sport, a game you like, an instrument you play, or something you enjoy doing with your family.

DATE:

Today I'm grateful for...

I'm grateful because...

Thank you, God, for...

We can be grateful for the ways God leads us throughout our lives. Read this verse about how God's Word, the Bible, guides us.

Your word is a lamp for my feet,
a light on my path.

PSALM 119:105 NIV

On the path below, write an instruction God gives to help us make good decisions.

DATE:

Today I'm grateful for...

I'm grateful because...

Thank you, God, for...

Happiness is contagious! Feeling the joy and positivity of others can uplift our own mood. Think of those you know who find joy in the small moments, and thank God for bringing them into your life as you add the finishing touches to these happy faces.

Love from the center of who you are . . .
Be good friends who love deeply . . .
Laugh with your happy friends when they're happy.

ROMANS 12:9–10,15 THE MESSAGE

DATE:

Today I'm grateful for...

I'm grateful because...

Thank you, God, for...

Keep track of what you're grateful for throughout your day and fill out the chart below.

	I am grateful for...	Because...
Morning		
Afternoon		
Evening		

DATE:

Today I'm grateful for...

I'm grateful because...

Thank you, God, for...

Fill in this heart with names of people you're thankful for.

DATE:

Today I'm grateful for...

I'm grateful because...

Thank you, God, for...

Things that are priceless can hold a lot of value—the kind of value that goes beyond what money can buy. Perhaps your priceless treasures include the warmth of your family's love, the laughter shared with friends, or the feeling of achieving a goal. Draw and write things below that are priceless to you.

How priceless is Your unfailing love, O God! People take refuge in the shadow of Your wings. They feast on the abundance of Your house; You give them drink from Your river of delights. For with You is the fountain of life; in Your light, we see light.

PSALM 36:7–9 NIV

DATE:

Today I'm grateful for...

I'm grateful because...

Thank you, God, for...

Read this Scripture about relationships and underline the words or phrases that stand out to you.

TWO PEOPLE ARE BETTER OFF THAN ONE,
FOR THEY CAN HELP EACH OTHER SUCCEED.
IF ONE PERSON FALLS, THE OTHER CAN
REACH OUT AND HELP. BUT SOMEONE WHO
FALLS ALONE IS IN REAL TROUBLE.

Ecclesiastes 4:9–10 NLT

Write down the name of a friend who has helped you. How could you show gratitude toward them?

Name:

How can I show gratitude?

DATE:

Today I'm grateful for...

I'm grateful because...

Thank you, God, for...

Circle the barnyard animal you are the most grateful for.

COW PIG SHEEP CHICKEN GOAT HORSE

MOUSE CAT DONKEY DUCK

Then, write down two reasons why you're grateful for this farm friend.

1.

2.

DATE:

Today I'm grateful for...

I'm grateful because...

Thank you, God, for...

Write about the holiday you are the most grateful for by filling in the blanks.

MY FAVORITE HOLIDAY IS ______________________.

I LOVE CELEBRATING THIS HOLIDAY BECAUSE

____

AND ____.

I GET READY FOR THIS HOLIDAY BY

________________________________. WHEN THIS

HOLIDAY COMES AROUND, I FEEL EXTRA GRATEFUL FOR

____.

SOMETHING I APPRECIATE ABOUT THIS HOLIDAY THAT

OTHER PEOPLE MIGHT NOT CARE ABOUT IS

____.

DATE:

Today I'm grateful for...

I'm grateful because...

Thank you, God, for...

Let's dive into the fascinating world of bugs! Imagine you are an explorer on a bug safari, and your mission is to draw all the amazing bugs you discover. What bugs do you find in your bug safari? Draw each bug carefully and, next to it, write or draw something you're grateful for that reminds you of that bug. For example, if you draw a busy bee, what in your life makes you as busy and joyful as a bee? Unleash your creativity and let the bug drawings become a colorful canvas of gratitude!

DATE:

Today I'm grateful for...

I'm grateful because...

Thank you, God, for...

Write a prayer thanking God
for a good gift He's given to you.

Every good and perfect gift is from above,
coming down from the Father of the heavenly lights,
who does not change like shifting shadows.

JAMES 1:17 NIV

DATE:

Today I'm grateful for...

I'm grateful because...

Thank you, God, for...

How grateful do you usually feel throughout your day? Fill in this pie chart to see a visual of how grateful, ungrateful, or neutral you feel.

○ Grateful ○ ungrateful ○ Neutral

BONUS

Look at the pie chart you filled out on Day 2 and compare it to the one from today. Do you think practicing gratitude has made a difference in how thankful you feel throughout a typical day?

DATE:

Today I'm grateful for...

I'm grateful because...

Thank you, God, for...

Color in this Bible verse.

ALWAYS BE JOYFUL.
NEVER STOP PRAYING.
BE THANKFUL IN
ALL CIRCUMSTANCES,
FOR THIS IS GOD'S WILL
FOR YOU WHO BELONG
TO CHRIST JESUS.

1 Thessalonians 5:16–18 NLT

DATE:

Today I'm grateful for...

I'm grateful because...

Thank you, God, for...

God made you in an amazing way! Write out 3–4 reasons why you're grateful for who you are.

The heavens declare the glory of God;
the skies proclaim the work of His hands.

PSALM 19:1 NIV

My First Gratitude Journal

First Edition, June 2024

Published by:

DaySpring

21154 Highway 16 East
Siloam Springs, AR 72761
dayspring.com

Written by: Amanda Jass
Cover Design and Illustrations by: Hannah Brinson

Printed in India
Prime: U2660
ISBN: 979-8-88602-859-1